We Can Be

The Radical Individualis[

By Robert Dean Lurie

Table of Contents:

Dedication

Introduction

Chapter I: Baby I dream

Chapter II: I, I will be king

Chapter III: I could make it all worthwhile

Chapter IV: It's no game

Chapter V: Immersed in Crowley's uniform

Chapter VI: You, you will be queen

Chapter VII: God is an American

Chapter VIII: Want an axe to break the ice

Chapter IX: All the young dudes

Epilogue

Liberty Island Media Group
New York, New York
www.LibertyIslandMag.com
©2016 Robert Dean Lurie
Designed by Meg Prom

For Joshua Will

"I can't tolerate people who want to form, or be part of, movements. It should always come back to individuals."
—David Bowie, 1977

"Integrity is the ability to stand by an idea. That presupposes the ability to think."
—Ayn Rand, *The Fountainhead*, 1943

Introduction

When rock star David Bowie died of cancer on January 10, 2016, the public outpouring of grief was more intense and widespread than for any other popular figure in recent memory. The *New York Times*, *CNN*, and *Rolling Stone* weighed in with the expected eulogies, but some of the more heartfelt tributes came from surprising corners of the cultural/political spectrum. William Doino, Jr., wrote movingly in *First Things* of Bowie's lifelong search for God. *National Review* called him "one of the last true Renaissance men." Noah Millman at *The American Conservative* wrote, "It seems off, somehow, that David Bowie should die at all, rather than be taken back up to his home planet on a beam of light and music." Even the Austrian School of Economics–oriented Mises Institute weighed in, praising Bowie's independent spirit and social-libertarian proclivities. Such unqualified praise from the conservative intelligentsia was, on the surface, surprising, given Bowie's longtime promotion of all manner of decadent behavior and what was called in his era "gender bending." But really, is it so hard to comprehend? Intelligence and talent still count for something, particularly now that those qualities are becoming rarer in the world of popular entertainment. Bowie unquestionably possessed both.

His was an impressive career by any measurement, spanning six decades of hit albums and a number of forays into theater, film, painting, and sculpture. Emerging into public consciousness in 1969 with the single "Space Oddity," David Bowie cycled through an impressive succession of genres: psychedelic folk, glam rock, proto-punk, "plastic soul," mainstream pop, hard rock, and techno, among others. In at least two instances he created entirely new genres that have yet to be properly named. Most impressive was the level of commitment he brought to each creative phase. He endured few fallow periods, and he proved remarkably adept at righting himself when he did fall into them.

Like any self-respecting rock-and-roller, Bowie pushed against social conventions at every turn. He conducted much of his rebellion with tongue firmly in cheek, but it had its desired effect. He retained the ability to shock and terrify right up through the final decade of his life: In 2013 YouTube temporarily removed his video for the song "The Next Day" for "violation of terms of service." Bowie must have enjoyed the situation, given that the video's offending nudity and gore drew their inspiration from the 14th-century novel cycle *The Decameron* and the Catholic legend of St. Lucy.

Bowie was always one step ahead of everyone. Smarter too, and better read. He thought way outside the box, and, in a world where everybody seems to serve somebody, or something else, he belonged only to himself. It is the purpose of this book to explore how, and why, David Bowie did it his way.

I

Baby I dream between the blade and the tongue
Of the rose on your cheek, the wounded and dumb

These lines, crooned out in a slinky reptilian voice over crashing drums, a loping bassline, and a guitar pattern that alternates between sharp, Stevie Ray Vaughan–style blues and outer-space reverb, comprise the opening salvo of Tin Machine, the 1989 debut album by the band of the same name featuring David Bowie on vocals, Reeves Gabrels on guitar, and the Sales brothers—Hunt and Tony—bringing up the rhythm section. The song is unabashedly about sex, but with lyrics like "Crucifix hangs / My heart's in my mouth," it stands out from such contemporary fare as Def Leppard's "Pour Some Sugar on Me."

These days, Tin Machine is not fondly remembered by many Bowie fans *or* critics. But something about the sheer audacity of the endeavor excites. It remains as one of the most radical about-faces ever made by a massively popular entertainer. Just a year prior, David Bowie had been traversing the planet peddling the overblown spectacle of the Glass Spider tour, which featured a stage crowded with bouncing eyeballs, hordes of dancers descending from the ceiling via ropes and pulleys, a slick backing band delivering unthreatening pop in carefully choreographed movements, and Bowie himself, prancing about in bright clothes with a head mic fastened to his overflowing blond mullet. Now, with Tin Machine, Bowie resurfaced in a brutal hard rock band that specialized in fuzzed-out, atonal noise of the Sonic Youth school. They played club gigs that leaned heavily toward improvisation. On any given night Tin Machine could scrape the ceiling of greatness or collapse into chaos.

Tin Machine could be considered one of David Bowie's "Howard Roark" moves. In Ayn Rand's popular but wildly polarizing novel *The Fountainhead*, Roark, the book's strong-willed protagonist, dynamites a housing complex he had designed in order to prevent it from getting compromised by third-party add-ons. In a metaphorical sense, Bowie dynamited his own career with the Tin Machine project, and it cost him considerably in the short term. Although a modest success in terms of sales, the band's stridently noncommercial debut led to a split between Bowie and his label, EMI. Furthermore, the follow-up albums *Tin Machine II* and *Oy Vey Baby* (a live set) literally bankrupted Victory Records, the band's subsequent label. Bowie's audience, too, abandoned him in droves.

Yet in a 2003 interview, one of Bowie's last in-depth conversations with a journalist prior to going publicly silent for the remainder of his life, the former architect of Tin Machine remained defiant. "I *love* Tin Machine," he told Paul Du Noyer of the U.K. magazine *The Word*. "It was a terrific experience...because now I felt I could make decisions about what I wanted to do over the coming years. There was nowhere to hide with that band. We had everything against us—and it was good!"

At surface level, Tin Machine was the height of career folly, and Bowie's intransigence in the face of widespread derision seemed to confirm the worst clichés of the "difficult artist." But at another level, it was an act of creative survival. Bowie had been here before. His action with Tin Machine was, in fact, the resurgence of a fiercely individualistic streak in his personality and art-making that had been present since the dawn of his career. In life, David Bowie tended to make his own rules. And creatively, he could be similarly fearless. "In art you can crash your plane and just walk away from it," he told a journalist, paraphrasing his friend and collaborator Brian Eno. For him, the crashing was crucial.

There is no direct evidence that David Bowie ever read *The Fountainhead*, though it is probable he did, given his lifelong love of books. Nor is there any evidence that Bowie ever felt any affinity for objectivism, the ethical, aesthetic, and political philosophy based around "laissez-faire capitalism" that Rand later developed and promulgated in works such as *Atlas Shrugged* and *The Virtue of Selfishness*. All things considered, it seems likely that Bowie would have had no truck with this group, given his disdain for movements in general and his lack of interest in politics and economic theory. But *The Fountainhead* is different from those later works in that it does not directly address politics or economics, focusing instead on the theme of individualism vs. collectivism. And through the character of Roark, the fiercely independent architect at the book's center, Rand presents a clear vision of what she considers the ideal artist hero: a creator who makes art exclusively for his own pleasure, who is not concerned with awards, critical reception, or even popular recognition, who doesn't waste time skirmishing with his adversaries because he doesn't think about them at all. Roark eschews the ordinary for the extraordinary, what is for what *ought to be.* This is a man concerned with the fortification of his own integrity rather than the acquisition of power. He takes what he wants from life, neither coercing others nor giving them undue consideration. He is the hero of his own journey, the sole judge of his own worth.

Roark is, of course, a fictional character, and a rather static one at that: He acts essentially the same at the end of *The Fountainhead* as he does at the beginning. David Bowie, of course, was *not* a cardboard cutout or stock literary character. He was, rather, a deeply divided human being. His fiercely independent streak had to contend not only with the external forces of societal constraints, rigid-minded record executives, and the expectations of his audience, but also with a strong internal craving for acceptance and popularity that often ran counter to his more radical impulses. Indeed, when Bowie took the extreme action of "dynamiting" his career with Tin Machine, the soul-enslaving compromise he was reacting against was largely one of his own making. In this perpetual inner battle, the better angels of his nature did not always win.

Nevertheless, in that rarified atmosphere occupied by the most successful popular entertainers of all time—artists such as Sinatra, The Beatles, The Rolling Stones, James Brown, Michael Jackson, and Madonna—David Bowie came closer to consistently embodying the Randian artist-hero ideal, as exemplified by the tenets listed above, than any other entertainer working at his level of success. It's also intriguing, on a superficial level at least, that Rand's description of Howard Roark as having a gaunt body, piercing eyes, and hair "the exact color of a ripe orange rind" conjures to mind David Bowie's alter-ego Ziggy Stardust without the makeup. In any case, the Howard Roark template, while rigid and not always applicable, can be a useful prism through which to view Bowie's career. David Bowie, quite simply, was the most radically individualistic popular entertainer we have ever seen. He took individualism to a place where he gave himself nearly complete artistic freedom, while still working within the bounds of taste and beauty. We don't get Howard Roarks in real life. But we did get David Bowie.

People responded to his fearlessness. "We can be heroes," Bowie sang: lines that resonated with an audience that comprised, in the words of biographer Christopher Sandford, "a whole generation of seekers who badly wanted a god, and found him." But the song "Heroes" is very different from the sort of crowd-pleasing anthem one typically hears from a rock artist. It is not a call to unify an arena full of sweaty concertgoers in some shared noble aim. Rather, it entreats each listener to break free of the herd. "['Heroes' is] compassionate for people and the silly desperate situations they've got themselves into," Bowie explained shortly after the song's release. "That we've *all* got ourselves into....Decisions to join or remain within sets of people. We haven't moved on at all from that tribal thing."

    For much of his career, David Bowie scrupulously avoided associating with causes of any kind. He harbored a deep-seated antipathy toward mass movements, even those which he himself founded and which he often tried to dismantle before they got out of control (hence his killing off of the Ziggy character in the mid-'70s). Yet Bowie couldn't help but become a "hero" to the freaks, the misfits, and the marginalized. In taking ownership of his perceived weaknesses—his awkwardness, his effeminate mannerisms, his mismatched eyes, his ambiguous sexuality—and celebrating them, *exaggerating* them, creating whole new personalities based around them, he gave others license to do the same. He offered an alternative definition of male "coolness," one that eschewed the macho swagger that had dominated up to that point, even—perhaps especially—in the realm of rock-and-roll, and replaced it with intelligence, outrageousness, and an embrace of the inner feminine. He did so because that was his correct way forward, the ideal method for a fundamentally shy kid from the London suburbs to project himself onto the world stage. Many of his listeners picked up on this lead. And while male fans were not required to wear makeup in order to heed their hero's call to celebrate themselves, the option was now officially on the table.

Bowie made similarly iconoclastic moves as a musical stylist. Feeling no connection with either the "give peace a chance"–style anthems of the preceding decade or the laid-back, groove-rock mentality of the current one, he cultivated a taut, muscular sound that counterbalanced his effeminate image. Bowie in the early 1970s *rocked*, particularly on the albums *The Man Who Sold the World*, *The Rise and Fall of Ziggy Stardust and the Spiders from Mars*, and *Aladdin Sane*. He was *not* the first glam rocker, but he was arguably the best—and indisputably the most successful. His best songs had a range and depth that transcended the genre. Lyrically, they mined philosophical and historical matter not often visited in the milieu of rock-and-roll. (I don't think you're going to find a lot of Nietzsche references on an Alice Cooper album, for instance.) And, as it turned out, this fascinating blend of styles was *not* the final destination but merely one stop in a long, shapeshifting journey.

So how did David Jones, the quiet, dreamy kid from Brixton, evolve into David Bowie, the flamboyant entertainer and champion of radical individualism? For clues, we must first cast our eyes back to his origins.

II

I, I will be king

In 1979, David Bowie sat down for a wide-ranging interview with Mavis Nicholson for the BBC program *Afternoon Plus*. For whatever reason, this appearance proved one of the few instances of his letting his guard down and giving some small glimpse of the man within. Suspended for the moment were the camp affectations, the animated gestures, and the strained, big-toothed grin and barking laugh he typically deployed during interviews. Instead, viewers were introduced to a quiet, thoughtful young man with a vigorous smoking habit.

Addressing the themes of isolation and loneliness that pervade much of his music, Bowie told Nicholson, "I think if [a person] is in isolation, instead of receiving the whole world as his home, he tends to create a micro world inside himself. And it's that peculiar part of the human mind that fascinates me: the small universes that can be created inside the mind." Bowie stated that he himself had never felt isolated, but that he often deliberately put himself into isolating situations—such as his move to Berlin in the late 1970s—in order to see what it felt like.

Here Bowie was being disingenuous. His biographers all agree that a sense of isolation had, in fact, been a key component of his psyche virtually from birth.

David Robert Jones was born in January 1947, the only child of Haywood Stenton "John" Jones and Margaret "Peggy" Burns. The parents did not enjoy an easy relationship. John was quiet and self-contained, whereas Peggy was a passionate extrovert, given to sudden mood swings. Furthermore, schizophrenia and other mental disorders afflicted her side of the family. The two parents quarreled often. David Jones felt the typical loneliness coupled with self-centeredness of an only child, compounded by a nagging fear that he might someday succumb to the family disease of madness. It was not an unfounded fear: Bowie's half-brother, Terry Burns, began showing signs of schizophrenia as a young adult and spent the remainder of his life in and out of institutions. Perhaps due to all of these circumstances, David Jones turned inward.

These were the obvious roots of his individuality, but there were more benign factors at play as well. Speaking of his family in a 1996 interview on Netherlands television, Bowie was able to look back with affection and credit their example for his own powerful self-reliant streak. "I don't think anybody in my family ever belonged to 'groups,'" he said. "We're not group people. We tend to be very self-sufficient people. Give us a book and a paintbrush and we don't really need anything else."

And here we arrive at the other major factor that shaped David Bowie's personality: his lifelong reading habit. In that same 1996 interview, he credited his father for his own love of reading. "To this day it still gives me the most extraordinary pleasure," he said. "I couldn't possibly tell you how fantastic it is to become fully involved in the thinking and the ideas and the location of somebody else's mind."

It was perhaps inevitable that the independent-minded young man would gravitate to writers of a similarly free-thinking disposition. An early touchstone was Jean Jacques Rousseau, whose works of political philosophy Jones/Bowie read as a teenager. We can only speculate on Bowie's takeaway from his reading of Rousseau's complex and varied writings. The idea of the "social contract"—that individuals should voluntarily subordinate some of their rights to the state in the interests of the "general will" or greater good—seems not to have made much of an impact on the young man at all, though it arguably assumed greater import as he grew older. Rousseau's advocacy of equality across class lines and his intriguing notion that "nature (makes) man happy and good, but that society depraves him and makes him miserable" probably found more favor. The latter sentiment surfaces, subtly but noticeably, on the albums *The Man Who Sold the World* and *Aladdin Sane*. Bowie would also have likely agreed with Rousseau's view that the sole aim of education ought to be to teach the individual how to reason.

The young Bowie also read the 19th-century German philosopher Friedrich Nietzsche. It would be difficult to overstate Nietzsche's influence on Bowie's work, as references—direct and oblique—to his ideas litter Bowie's first several albums. Nietzsche is perhaps best known for having declared in his book *The Gay Science* that "God is dead," which has often been interpreted as a call to atheism. The philosopher's actual views, however, may have been more complicated. In her 1968 introduction to a reissued version of *The Fountainhead*, Ayn Rand described Nietzsche as a "mystic." She intended this as a pejorative (she also described him as an "irrationalist"), but her own bias against such things should not detract from the fundamental correctness of her interpretation. The "God is dead" declaration more accurately heralds the death of traditional metaphysics. It is true that Nietzsche himself had no faith in religion or traditional notions of a deity, and from that flowed a negation of traditional morality, but his faith in *art*—and in music in particular—as an acceptable replacement could almost be termed religious.

Nihilism, the view that life is both meaningless and valueless, often accompanies an initial loss of religious faith. But Nietzsche rejected this position as well. A useful generalization of his work would be to think of it as a long-form grappling with how we may best approach life in the wake of the collapse of the old value systems. The solution, in Nietzsche's view, is not to give in to chaos and despair but to embrace the world *as it is* with vitality and joy, and to create new values based on the particular needs of the moment. Nietzsche eschewed fashionable ideas of egalitarianism in favor of a recognition of man's fundamentally unequal nature: that human beings have differing levels of strength, intelligence, talent, and ability. Certain individuals will inevitably rise from the herd, realizing their potential more completely, more definitively, than others. These are the beings who will shape the new values. These are "the Supermen." Through the force of their "will to power," they assume their rightful place as leaders and innovators and push humanity forward. In Nietzsche's view, this ascendancy should be encouraged, not stymied.

Obviously, this philosophy is ripe for misinterpretation, and Bowie himself, perhaps addled by heavy cocaine use, would take Nietzsche's ideas to disturbing, fascistic extremes in the mid-1970s. But initially it was the affirming, romantic aspects of the Superman ideal that held him in thrall. Subsequent events indicate that he saw the concept as an invitation, a permission, for his own self-actualization. He certainly had plenty of time to think about these things during the eight-month period he spent away from school in his mid-teens recovering from an injury—incurred during a "fight over a girl"—that left his left eye permanently disfigured. "I took a look at my thoughts, my appearance, my expressions, my mannerisms and idiosyncrasies and didn't like them," he later told *Rolling Stone*. "So I stripped myself down, chucked things out and replaced them with a completely new personality." It could be said that David Jones read Nietzsche and concluded that "we can be heroes." David Jones subsequently became David Bowie, a change in moniker that was one-half necessitated by the emergence of another performer with his name (the Monkees' Davy Jones) and one-half mandated by his new Nietzsche-derived sense of self-empowerment. "The name Bowie just appealed to me when I was younger," he told *Rolling Stone* in 1974. "I was into a kind of heavy philosophy thing when I was 16 years old, and I wanted a truism about cutting through the lies and all that."

III

I could make it all worthwhile as a rock and roll star

The will to power asserted itself early on. At the age of 12, David Jones confessed to a schoolteacher his ambition to become "the British Elvis." In 1969, well before he had experienced major success, the recently minted David Bowie told journalist (and future biographer) George Tremlett, "I shall be a millionaire by the time I'm 30." This serene confidence in his own destiny had already carried the young musician though a succession of managers and failed bands, and would continue to guide him in the fitful years ahead. How much of this derived from Nietzsche is not clear; his "Elvis" comment predates his discovery of the philosopher. But Nietzsche's ideas definitely bolstered, and clarified, such ambitions.

David Bowie wrestled somewhat with Nietzsche on the question of God, though it's possible that Nietzsche helped nudge the young man away from the safe route of traditional religion in favor of an individual (and, as it turned out, lifelong) search for the true shape of the divine.

Bowie most assuredly did not believe that God was dead. On the contrary, he made the cryptic pronouncement in the song "Width of a Circle" that "God's a young man too." Later, he described the search for God as his primary motivating impulse in life and art. "Everything I've written is about 'Who is my God?'" he said. "How does he show himself? What is my higher stage, my higher being?"—thus marrying his

Nietzschean ideas of self-actualization to a spiritual quest. He told Paul Du Noyer, "If you can make the spiritual connection with some kind of clarity then everything else would fall into place. A morality would seem to be offered, a plan would seem to be offered. Some sense would be there. But it evades me. Yet I can't help writing about it." What may have frustrated him in life evidently fueled his art, as his ongoing failure in finding a satisfactory resolution in this realm lent his music a restless, searching quality right to the end.

Rounding out Bowie's early influences was his discovery, via his half brother, Terry Burns, of the American "Beat" writer Jack Kerouac, whose *On the Road* blends the Nietzschean celebration of self with the sort of rapturous, open-ended spirituality that Bowie sought in his own life. *This* spirituality somehow fused Kerouac's ingrained Catholicism to the delirious energy of Charlie Parker's saxophone playing. In the cascading torrent of notes, Kerouac heard rhythms and possibilities which became, for him, the pulse to a different mode of living. It was the same effect that the music of Little Richard later had on the young Bowie: the wildness, the promise of music—in this case rock-and-roll—as a means of deliverance from the emotional and spiritual constraints of a lower-middle-class life. Kerouac had captured the seismic upheaval of the arrival of rock-and-roll, minus the rock, several years early.

Even with the advent of the hippie movement in the 1960s, David Bowie always remained a Beat partisan, or, rather, a fan of two particular Beats—Kerouac and William S. Burroughs, which is significant. Despite the presence of Allen Ginsberg—a more overtly "activist" type—in both movements, the Beats were by and large an apolitical group. They were less concerned with remaking society than with living under its radar, or, barring that, carving out some sense of individuality within society's constraints. With Kerouac, Bowie shared an ambivalence toward revolutionary action. This is borne out by the song "Cygnet Committee" from his early album *Space Oddity*, which takes direct aim at the groupthink aspects of the hippie movement. "I ravaged at my finance just for those / Those whose claims were steeped in peace, tranquility," he sings. Later, he mocks the violent tendencies of many of these supposed peace activists: "I will fight for the right to be right / I will kill for the good of the fight for the right to be right." The communal aspects of hippie culture disturbed Bowie. During a joint interview with Burroughs in 1974, Bowie spoke derisively about anything that smacked of the hippie ethos, including the typical rock concert experience. "The idea of getting minds together smacks of the Flower Power period to me," Bowie said. "The coming together of people I find obscene as a principle. It is not human. It is not a natural thing as some people would have us believe." He went on to lambast sci-fi/libertarian hero Robert Heinlein's novel *Stranger in a Strange Land*, whose alien-messiah protagonist, Valentine Michael Smith, was often thought to be a point of reference for Bowie's Ziggy Stardust character, as being "terrible" and "a bit too Flower-Powery." In another interview, Bowie reiterated the counter-revolutionary themes of "Cygnet Committee":

I would like to believe that people knew what they were fighting for and why they wanted a revolution, and exactly what it was within that they didn't like. I mean to put down a society or the aims of the society is to put down a hell of a lot of people, and that scares me—that there should be such a division where one set of people are saying that another should be killed. You know you can't put down anybody. You can just try and understand. The emphasis shouldn't be on revolution, it should be on communication.

IV

It's no game

    Readers detecting a certain conservative strain in Bowie's comments here are not imagining things, though Bowie himself would almost certainly never have used such a term to describe himself. Complementing, and not infrequently contradicting, Bowie's prevailing social-libertarian worldview was a certain reticence toward social disruption not too dissimilar from the philosophy of 18th-century politician and writer Edmund Burke, though it ought to be stressed here that Bowie's feelings in this regard were likely intuitive rather than the result of any careful consideration. Burke famously broke from contemporaries and condemned the French Revolution, correctly predicting that its Rousseau-inspired call to equality and social redistribution at the point of a bayonet would lead to chaos and atrocity on a mass scale. Popular historian Will Durant succinctly sums up Burke's primary point as being that, in history, "the brakes are often just as important as the gas."

    This is not to suggest that Bowie read Burke in depth, though he was likely familiar with his ideas. Nor is it to suggest that Bowie saw parallels between Burke's political philosophy and aspects of his own life. It is only to point out that there are a number of "stations" across the continuum of the philosophical right: radical liberty, or freedom, positioned at one end; Burke's careful balancing of forward movement against the lessons of history and tradition inhabiting the middle; and at the other extreme an impulse toward authoritarianism that can devolve into fascism. At various points during his career, particularly in the 1970s, Bowie passed through each of these mindsets. There seemed to be some pretty serious cognitive dissonance occurring in 1976, when Bowie simultaneously flirted with ideas of Aryan supremacy while carrying on numerous affairs with black women while also recording an album, *Station to Station*, infused with Jewish mysticism. There is a lesson to be learned here: playing personal host to a rather extreme marketplace of ideas while subsisting only on cocaine and milk is bound to destabilize one's psyche. But if the pivot to fascism constituted a surprising and alarming development, it at least had identifiable roots in Bowie's earlier preoccupation with Nietzsche. Taken in the context of the ego-distorting, funhouse mirror world of the rock star, you can almost see how he got from point A to point B, even if you want to look away from it as from a particularly nasty automobile accident. At any rate, after a couple of ill-advised Hitler salutes and an interview in which Bowie speculated on his chances of becoming England's first fascist prime minister, he went back to the ideological drawing board and re-emerged with a sensible antipathy toward political absolutes.

> A number of years later, Bowie summarized his feelings on politics: I think that unless one has a penetrating understanding of the social issues of the time it's very dangerous to get involved in other areas where one might be misled by forces who would take you off the path. It's very important not to

be led, and in political areas I think it's very dodgy for a lot of artists—including myself—who have only an understanding of the topsoil of the political and social system to declare themselves under any political banner.

This remained his default public setting for the remainder of his career. Privately he identified as a liberal, though it is intriguing that his longtime friend Gary Oldman, the actor and noted conservative, listed Bowie and conservative commentator Charles Krauthammer as two individuals who "speak the truth in this culture" during his infamous PC-bashing interview with *Playboy* in 2014. Oldman was primarily speaking here of Bowie's artistic autonomy, and how that afforded Bowie the ability to convey his personal truth, but it seems at least possible that in his pairing of Bowie with Krauthammer, Oldman was also thinking of his friend's lifelong refusal to adhere to accepted wisdom in all realms, including politics.

Bowie clearly shared at least some of Edmund Burke's views on revolution and mass-movement idealism, and privately he occasionally fretted about the excesses of his own libertine lifestyle. When informed by his first wife, Angela, that they were expecting a child, Bowie wondered aloud whether Haddon Hall, the rented mansion where the Bowies, along with a menagerie of transitory lovers of both genders, seemingly spent their days re-enacting the entirety of the Kama Sutra along with passages of de Sade, might be an "awkward" environment for the raising of his son. This brief intrusion of common sense proved more an exception than the norm during this period, however.

Bowie's privately conservative—or, if you'd prefer, conventional—side was recently explored in depth by no less an authority than his biographer Christoper Sandford in a tribute piece for *The American Conservative* titled "Thin Right Duke," wherein Sandford called attention to Bowie's "flagrantly unfashionable belief in sound traditional values such as those he called 'self-denial, discipline and constant graft,' along with a refreshing ability to get through lengthy autobiographical interviews without whining, blaming, or emoting." Over a subsequent email exchange, Sandford elaborated on this aspect of Bowie's personality:

> I know the words "conservative" and "ordinary" aren't the ones that normally leap to mind when discussing DB, but I always got that impression of him. I remember several people telling me how even at the nadir/zenith of the coked-out Thin White Duke days his fundamental idea of a good time was to sit alone watching British sitcoms on TV, and/or to curl up with a good book.

Obviously, the label of "ordinary" may seem at first to complicate our radical-individualist thesis. But it need not. Sandford's own book on Bowie, *Loving the Alien*, is filled with tales of his subject "fucking everything that moved and quite a lot that didn't," sniffing cocaine at boardroom meetings, exorcising malevolent swimming pools, and storing his own urine in a refrigerator to ward off spirits and/or vampires. These are not behaviors that one would typically ascribe to a "conservative" or "ordinary" man. But Bowie himself may have cleared up the apparent discrepancy by describing himself to *Esquire* as "a librarian with a sex drive." Setting aside the entirely unfair aspersions that formulation casts on actual librarians, and factoring out drug psychosis (which likely contributed to the more outlandish non-sexual behaviors listed above), that one sentence does a fairly good job of making peace between the two poles of his personality. Bowie was, essentially, a quiet, bookish man possessed of a powerful sexual urge, one which, due to his tremendous success, he found himself uniquely positioned to indulge. Cocaine fortified his nerves in engaging with the external world, though it also contributed to behaviors that we might call "batshit crazy."

In the public arena the "conservative" aspects Sandford noted rarely asserted themselves. When they did, the effect could be memorable and sometimes jarring. An early indicator of this side of Bowie came in "Word on a Wing," an unabashed plea to the Christian God nestled alongside the otherwise Kabbalistic and occult-preoccupied songs that comprised the *Station to Station* LP from 1976. "Lord, I kneel and offer you my word on a wing," Bowie sang. "And I'm trying hard to fit among your scheme of things." Then there was the apparently spontaneous moment at a Freddie Mercury tribute concert in 1992 when Bowie fell to his knees and recited the Lord's Prayer to a bewildered audience, his voice choking up on the words "forgive us our trespasses." In moments like these, particularly given

Bowie's wild image, the conventional became radical. There are few gestures more shocking in the Dionysian world of rock-and-roll than that of one of the perceived agents of society's downfall humbling himself—not before his audience but before the God of his forebears—and offering up an explicitly sectarian prayer. Madonna's dance in front of burning crosses in her "Like a Prayer" video pales in comparison. In an interview with *Rolling Stone* the following year, Bowie acknowledged that the gesture had surprised his listeners that night. "But," he added, "it wasn't for them."

V

Immersed in Crowley's uniform

In a 1980 piece for *New Musical Express*, Angus MacKinnon described David Bowie as "one of the most profoundly amoral people I've met." That statement made for good copy, but it's hard to know exactly what MacKinnon meant, especially given the qualities noted above. Bowie had always adhered to a moral code, though at times he chose one that large swathes of mainstream society found abhorrent. Given Bowie's ingrained sense of independence, fortified by those early influences of Nietzsche and Kerouac (not to mention the siren's calls of Little Richard and Fats Domino), it was not at all surprising that he developed idiosyncratic values—particularly in the area of sexual relations.

In this regard he was bolstered by another powerful influence: the English occultist Aleister Crowley (1875–1947). Some readers may be familiar with the legends surrounding Crowley: outlandish tales of animal sacrifice, black magic, prodigious drug abuse, and sexual deviance of every conceivable stripe. Many of the stories are true, and it's hard to get past them. Per various accounts, the collateral damage from Crowley's lifelong vision quest included at least two cats (presumably black), a couple of goats who happened to be in the wrong place at the wrong time, a crucified toad, an unlucky acolyte who expired after drinking contaminated cat's blood, and a boatload of wives, mistresses, and male lovers who ended up either dead by their own hand or institutionalized. There is also the matter of Crowley's claim to be the channel for a powerful dark spirit called Aiwass who had a bracing message for humanity at the dawn of the Age of Horus. It's a lot to take in. Yet the fact remains that if you have an affinity for Nietzsche and/or Ayn Rand's idea of the ego as "fountainhead" for man's progress rather than as an impediment to be overcome, and would also like to see some form of spirituality brought back into the mix, Crowley fills a gap. Consider the following passage from Crowley's *Liber Oz* manifesto, written near the end of his life in 1941:

> Man has the right to think what he will:
> to speak what he will:
> to write what he will:
> to draw, paint, carve, etch, mould, build as he will:
> to dress as he will.

Read on its own, independent of the details of Crowley's life or the occult methodology underpinning his belief system, it enjoys considerable common ground with both Ayn Rand and Nietzsche. A later passage would have had special relevance for Bowie:

> Man has the right to love as he will:—
> "take your fill and will of love as ye will,
> when, where, and with whom ye will." —AL.
> I. 51

Crowley devised a shorthand for his belief system—"Do what thou wilt shall be the whole of the law"—which he somewhat disconcertingly used to begin and end every conversation. (There was apparently no "Hey, how's it going?" when talking with Crowley.) Richard Kaczynski, author of the authoritative Crowley biography *Perdurabo*, sums up the phrase thusly:

> "Do what thou wilt..." simply means find out what you're here to do, and do nothing else. It's about finding the thing that you love. Don't get discouraged; see it through to the end. That's what Crowley's magical name Perdurabo means: "I shall endure to the end." Concomitant with that, other people don't have the right to tell you what you can or cannot do if you're not bothering anyone else. I think that's a message we can all find inspiring.

Directly and indirectly, Crowley and Nietzsche became a sort of double act in Bowie's work, popping up on the early albums *The Man Who Sold the World*, *Hunky Dory*, and *Station to Station*. The Crowley influence receded from view after that, though *Rolling Stone* has noted that the video for "Blackstar," the title track from Bowie's final album, appears to nod to the occultist.

Bowie's typical approach was to scatter philosophical references throughout his lyrics in a sort of Dadaist spray, relying on the music to create bridges between ideas that might otherwise seem disparate. Thus, 1970's "Width of a Circle" begins with an overt homage to Nietzsche's *Beyond Good and Evil: Prelude to a Philosophy of the Future*, then proceeds, somewhat incongruously, to namecheck the poet Kahlil Gibran, and finishes with a Crowleyesque tale of a homoerotic encounter with God. (Or is it the Devil?)

"Quicksand," from the 1971 album *Hunky Dory*, contains perhaps the most vivid juxtaposition of the two men's ideas. The song begins with the line "I'm closer to the Golden Dawn, immersed in Crowley's uniform of imagery": a reference to The Hermetic Order of the Golden Dawn, an early-20th-century "secret society" whose membership roll included Crowley, poets William Butler Yeats and A.E. Waite, and novelist Algernon Blackwood. Later, Bowie declares that he is "not a prophet," but rather "a mortal with potential of a superman"—an obvious nod to Nietzsche.

Given the prominence of these two champions of the human ego in the song's verses, the first line of the chorus, "Don't believe in yourself / Don't deceive with belief," puzzles. What did Bowie believe in if not himself? Yet if we read "Quicksand" as the document of a roiling internal debate, a vivid depiction of its author's "sinking in the quicksand of [his] thought," a meaning begins to coalesce. Bowie's natural inclination to exalt the self sometimes came into conflict with a Buddhist-derived urge to obliterate the self completely. In Bowie's life the former impulse tended to hold sway, though in "Quicksand" the conflict remains unresolved. We are assured that "knowledge comes with death's release," a sentiment Bowie may have intended to be uplifting.

In "Oh! You Pretty Things" (also on *Hunky Dory*), the Nietzschean and Crowleyan impulses prevail. "Let me make it plain," Bowie sings. "Gotta make way for the homo superior"—a sly nod both to Nietzsche's "Superman" concept and Bowie's emerging reputation as a sexual provocateur. And yet, even in this song of apparent triumph, an ominous reference to "a crack in the sky and a hand reaching down to me" sounds an off-note.

This same dichotomy subtly permeates Bowie's two most overtly anthemic compositions of the era: "Changes" and "All the Young Dudes." He refers to himself as "the faker" in the former, and in the latter asks, "Is there concrete all around or is it in my head?" Thus, even in songs that ostensibly rallied for liberation, Bowie could rarely get all his oars going in the same direction. He staged revolts against his own revolts. This made him a less-than-satisfactory messiah, but a most intriguing artist.

He knew what he was doing. One-dimensional anthems tend to make an immediate splash but then fade from memory. Bowie's songs almost always include hints of an internal struggle to mirror the external forces roiling against their "heroes." And for that reason, they tend to stick with the listener longer.

There is at least one exception to this rule: 1974's "Rebel Rebel," which glories in a total liberation from conventional morality with no hint of doubt or negative consequence. The searing defiance of its lyrics, married to a spiky guitar riff that, to paraphrase a Buddhist koan, seemed to embody the face of rock-and-roll before rock-and-roll was born, ensured its immortality. Here, "Do what thou wilt" did indeed become "the whole of the law."

If "Rebel Rebel" was the exterior, musical manifestation of Crowley's dictum in Bowie's life, how did the ideas play out in the private sphere? The reality was complicated. In some respects Bowie's personal life could come across like rollicking, debauched outtakes from *This Is Spinal Tap*, as on the morning in 1970 when the young singer awoke, fresh from engaging in a threesome with his girlfriend Angela Barnett and another woman and proceeded to escort Barnett down to the courthouse to make an honest woman of her. It was an unconventional beginning to a most unconventional marriage that would generate chaos and creative catalyst in equal measure—until it didn't. Perhaps only the 1970s could have accommodated such a union, and so it seems fitting that Bowie and Barnett's divorce was finalized at the decade's end.

One can read of the details of the Bowies' wide-open marriage and feel a certain grudging admiration for the sheer audacity of the whole enterprise. *Those crazy kids...flying too close to the sun, thinking they could have it all, in every which way, all the time. How could it not come crashing down in flames?*

But in the midst of their riotously lived "song of the '70s," some darker notes sounded. Just a few days after David Bowie's death, a number of online pieces began circulating that rehashed the story of Lori Maddox, a onetime groupie who claimed to have lost her virginity to David Bowie in the early 1970s when she was just 14 years old[1] and he was in his mid-20s. Although this information has been in circulation for years, the blogosphere predictably treated it as a shocking new revelation, one piece describing Bowie as a "monster" and an "abuser" and another churning over his "child rape" problem. A well-meaning blogger/activist named Louise Pennington stated that she would no longer be buying Bowie's music. The unfortunate truth, though, is that if Pennington wants to screen her listening choices based on whether or not the artist engaged in sex with minors, she will also need to avoid The Beatles, The Rolling Stones, The Who, Led Zeppelin, The Eagles, Rod Stewart, and The Stooges. For whatever reason, a porous definition of the age of consent was an embedded facet of rock-and-roll culture in the 1950s, '60s and '70s, and poked its head into the 1980s with Winger's "Seventeen." The Knack's hugely popular 1979 hit "My Sharona" glorified "the touch of the younger kind." Complicating the predator/victim narrative in the specific case of David Bowie is the fact that the adult Maddox is apparently happy, well-adjusted, and proud of her experience with the older rock star. That didn't stop countless bloggers from declaring her a victim anyway, but Rebecca Vipond Brink of *The Frisky* sounded a note of feminist dissension: "I fail to see how telling a woman's story for her advances women's autonomy. Age of consent laws don't exist for bloggers or interested parties on social media to tell women decades after the fact, 'you're a victim whether or not you believe that to be true.'"

This is not meant in any way to excuse Bowie's actions. Viewed through the lens of fatherhood, it is difficult to imagine any parent—in the 1970s or any other modern era—being comfortable with the idea of their 14-year-old daughter getting seduced by an older musician. And it is truly a disturbing experience, at least from our current vantage point, to view photos of the barely pubescent Maddox arm in arm with the much-older Jimmy Page, her subsequent lover after Bowie. These men clearly knew better.

More disturbing, in this writer's view, than the Maddox story are the many other tales dating from this era of women's debasing themselves in their efforts to get to Bowie, and of Bowie apparently encouraging such behavior. We are talking here of the all-too-common rock cliché of roadies and bodyguards dangling the prospect of backstage access as an exchange for sex. In some instances, Bowie allegedly strode in while a bodyguard was having sex with a groupie and took the man's place mid-coitus. While this sort of thing is par for the course in histories of other, more boorish rock stars, it seems jarring here, given Bowie's refined image and supposed sensitivity to fragile souls.

This is the dark side of "Do what thou wilt." Bowie seemed to move through the early 1970s as a force of pure sexual will, using the body of each lover as he saw fit, then discarding her (or him; Maddox describes Bowie as being "totally bisexual" at this time) in favor of the next one. While there is always a danger in imposing moral judgment on people and events in a bygone era, it is difficult not to read a certain amount of contempt in Bowie's actions, even if he did not seem to act with any conscious malice.

Jimmy Page, for his part, remains unrepentant about *all* of his past deeds—which in some respects is a refreshing stance, given the overly confessional, hand-wringing nature of our modern era. But there is some evidence that David Bowie did come to regret the darker aspects of his libertine youth. The clues appear primarily in song. In 1991 a track called "Shopping For Girls" (from the second Tin Machine album) dealt pointedly with the epidemic of child prostitution in Thailand. "Gaze down into her eyes for a million miles," Bowie sings. "Wanna give her a name and a clean rag doll." While the girls in the song were considerably younger than the groupies he had bedded, the vacant stares and conditions of "dull cold eyes" and "mind unstable"—in both the girls *and* the johns in the narrative—were qualities with which Bowie would have been intimately familiar.

In 2011 Bowie recorded a powerful track intended for his *Next Day* album called "God Bless the Girl," which seemed to examine the life situation of a sex worker from all angles. We are told that the song's protagonist, Jacqui, "loves her work, and her work is love," yet she is "too afraid to run away / like a slave without chains." The unnamed narrator keeps repeating "I don't wanna hurt you / I just wanna have some fun." If the younger Bowie had been willfully blind to all aspects of his impersonal sexual transactions other than his own pleasure, the older Bowie, to whom karma had delivered a daughter late in life, seemed to grasp the whole picture. How completely he may have reconciled this new awareness with his own past remains, appropriately, a private affair. The songs tell us what we need to know.

VI

You, you will be queen

    David Bowie composed much of the material for *The Man Who Sold the World* and *Hunky Dory* in a relative vacuum. During the period between his initial splash of success with the "Space Oddity" single in 1969 and his eventual breakthrough with 1972's *The Rise and Fall of Ziggy Stardust and the Spiders From Mars*, the songwriter struggled to find an audience—even as his material became more and more assured. He knew early on that he wanted to incorporate flamboyance into his visual image, but early attempts did not seem to click. In what is perhaps the single most "Spinal Tap" moment of this story, Bowie's long-term musical cohort Tony Visconti walked backstage after a "tarted-up" performance with Bowie at the Roundhouse in 1970 to find that his civilian clothes had been stolen. Thus, after enduring jeers from an audience hostile to Bowie and company's camped-out approach to rock-and-roll, Visconti was forced to ride the public bus home wearing a full-bodied glittering white jumpsuit and cape. This early humiliation may have nudged Visconti into assuming an exclusively behind-the-scenes production role on future Bowie projects.
    But the man at the center of the stage remained undeterred. Bowie next raised eyebrows by wearing a "man's dress" during a press tour of America in 1971. As audacious as that might have seemed at the time, particularly in the "flyover country" areas of the United States, it could not have prepared anyone in either the U.S. or the U.K. for the spectacle of Ziggy Stardust—

Bowie's otherworldly, aggressively extroverted alter ego resplendent in brightly colored form-hugging Kabuki costumes and a spiky orange haircut. He was an alien messiah peddling "hazy cosmic jive" whose primary message was: "Let all the children boogie."

Ziggy made his biggest initial splash during a performance of the song "Starman" on the BBC's *Top of the Pops* in 1972. One of the many viewers tuning in that night was a young Christopher Sandford, who still remembers the event vividly. "England in the early '70s truly was pretty bleak on just about every material level," he says now.

> I remember it as an era of power cuts, tinned Spam, freezing bedrooms, and one's parents constantly (and, in retrospect, rightly) fretting about making ends meet. So when one dark Thursday night this impossibly exotic creature appeared, as it were out of the blue, dressed like Lauren Bacall and trilling "Starman" on *Top of the Pops*, it was truly a, or the, proverbial water-cooler event for those of us aged anywhere between about 8-20.

In some respects the Ziggy Stardust character served a very practical purpose for Bowie. Ziggy allowed Bowie to fully embrace all the contrivances of the typical rock performance—the sweeping gestures, florid outpourings of emotion, and exhortations to the crowd to "give me your hands 'cause you're wonderful"—without embarrassment. He was able to set aside his reticence toward "getting minds together" because he viewed each performance by Ziggy and the Spiders as a stage enactment of the loose narrative from the album. The audiences, however, missed the fact that this narrative culminated with Ziggy's ultimate destruction by the forces he had unleashed. It seems Bowie did his job too well; the glittery Ziggy came off like an explosion of Technicolor across an otherwise monochrome England. And in an America numbed by the continuing Vietnam conflict and the emerging Watergate scandal, he provided an engaging distraction for some and a way forward for others. The latter outcome was not exactly what Bowie had intended, but it certainly didn't hurt sales.

How should we view Ziggy Stardust today? Was he simply a character, assumed and then discarded by Bowie the actor in the manner of a role in a play? Or was he an important cultural touchstone, a leader of a new sexual revolution and harbinger of our current churnings over gender identity and LGBTQ rights? Bowie spent many years emphasizing the former and downplaying or ignoring the latter. In an interview for German media in 1978, Bowie insisted that he had never been a leader of any sort and that the youth anthems of the Ziggy era were simply "the characters singing." In the book *Bowie: Loving the Alien*, Christopher Sandford documents Bowie's mounting anxiety at audiences' tendency to take the messianic aspects of the storyline a bit too literally. Such concerns played a part in Bowie's decision to pull the plug on the character and disband the Spiders in 1973.

"Ziggy" can also be viewed as an amplification of certain aspects of Bowie's personality. The drug use and sexual experimentation were already well-ingrained qualities, but what Ziggy discarded was the reticent side—the John Jones factor—that had tended to keep those things in check. The persona served as an invitation, and an excuse, for Bowie to indulge his id without consequence. In subsequent years, Bowie often made statements to the effect that "the character took over." A number of journalists blithely go along with this narrative. But the character didn't really take David Bowie anywhere he hadn't yearned to go.

This is what Ziggy meant to Bowie, but it can be argued that such concerns are less relevant here than at any other point in Bowie's career, for Ziggy Stardust took on a life of his own and came to mean more to the public than all of Bowie's other characters combined. Bowie ought not to have been surprised, for Ziggy rode to prominence on the back of an infamous *Melody Maker* interview during which Bowie (or Ziggy?) declared, "I'm gay, and always have been, even when I was David Jones." The effect on popular culture was immediate. Homosexuality was not a new development in rock-and-roll, but no performer had ever flaunted it so openly and unapologetically. Bowie's revelation, if we may call it that, was an exceptionally brave gesture—and a huge gamble; as Sean Egan, editor of the book *Bowie on Bowie: Interviews and Encounters*, notes, "even most hippies and rock consumers were repulsed by homosexuality at the time." But the gamble paid off: the *Melody Maker* piece catapulted the heretofore obscure songwriter onto the public stage and resulted in his music's getting heard by hundreds of thousands of newly curious ears. He became the talk of the pop music world overnight. And, for a previously marginalized segment of the population, his name became a rallying cry. "For gay musicians, Bowie was seismic," singer Tom Robinson declared. "To hell with whether he disowned us later."

Ah yes, the second part...

The young Bowie ought to have foreseen the years of explaining and clarifying he had in store, given his noted appetite for women. But he probably couldn't help himself; the immediate payoff was far too tempting. "I'm gay" makes a much bigger splash than "I'm primarily heterosexual but I like to experiment and affect gay mannerisms." And anyway, his statement contained at least some truth, if not the whole truth. Bowie *had* engaged in homosexual relationships, and would continue to do so—at least through 1976. He could legitimately claim to be bisexual, even if his growing docket of partners remained overweighted on the female side.

But perhaps inevitably, Bowie came to regard his gay-icon role as a limitation, even if that role had put him on the public radar in the first place. Thus, in the early 1980s he began a long, tortured, and ultimately futile attempt to extricate himself from the implications of his own prior statements. He told *Rolling Stone*'s Kurt Loder that the *Melody Maker* declaration had been the biggest mistake he had ever made. In other interviews, he quipped that he was a "closet heterosexual," or a "trisexual": "I'll try anything—once." He said to David Sinclair in 1993, "I didn't ever feel that I was a real bisexual...I was physical about it, but frankly it wasn't enjoyable. It was almost like I was testing myself." These statements come across about as disingenuous as his original self-outing; after all, no one put a gun to his head in 1972 and told him to have sex with men. But another statement in the Sinclair piece is perhaps more telling:

> Remember, in the early 1970s [homosexuality] was still virtually taboo. There might have been free love, but it was heterosexual love. I like this twilight world. I like the idea of these clubs and these people and everything about it being something that nobody knew anything about. So it attracted me like crazy.

Bowie had a vested interest in gay culture's remaining edgy and subversive—and underground; he found it useful to his identity as a rebellious rock star—which makes him a problematic figure in the larger gay rights movement. We have no way of knowing what he thought of the efforts in our modern era to normalize gay relationships and make them an almost mundane, accepted part of life—to the point where gay partnerships come to mirror heterosexual ones, down to the institution of marriage. Given his brief but relatively serious relationship with the transgender nightclub singer Romy Haag in the mid-1970s, it seems reasonable to assume that Bowie would have supported transgender rights, but on this and all such questions he remained publicly silent. He also refused all entreaties from leaders in the LGBTQ community to speak out on behalf of the movement's concerns. On the issue of gay rights, as with so many others, Bowie's concern began and ended with a desire for greater freedom of individual behavior. The only rallies he ever participated in were those he led from the stage in the character of Ziggy. "Give me your hands—'cause you're wonderful." That was enough for most people.

VII

God is an American

Many of the intellectual influences we have examined up to this point—Nietzsche, Kerouac, Crowley, and others—dominated David Bowie's music and actions during the pivotal decade of the 1970s but faded from view shortly thereafter. Not so for William S. Burroughs, godfather of the Beat movement, lifelong outlaw—literary and otherwise—and perhaps the most radical individualist of them all. The Burroughs influence held sway over Bowie from the mid-1970s, if not earlier, up until the end of the singer's life. During the Earthling tour in 1997, a huge flickering image of Burroughs, superimposed over an American flag, appeared every night on the backing screen as Bowie sang the line "God is an American" (from "I'm Afraid of Americans").

As a role model, William Burroughs is arguably a more problematic figure than even Crowley. A lifelong drug addict and sexual iconoclast who frequently sought out male partners well below the age of consent, Burroughs famously shot his wife dead in Mexico City in 1951 during a bizarre drinking game and then skipped town while on bail. (He was convicted, in absentia, of homicide.) In spite of such behaviors, which put him well outside both the bounds of acceptable society and the law itself, Burroughs nevertheless managed to get elected to the prestigious American Academy and Institute of Arts and Letters in 1983—perhaps his most subversive achievement, given his unapologetically renegade life and the frequently unsettling nature of his writing.

Bowie seems to have been most drawn to Burroughs's "cut-up" method: a technique (literally cutting up linear text and re-arranging the words at random in search of provocative new juxtapositions) "discovered" by artist Brion Gysin and subsequently developed by Burroughs. A strong argument can be made that cut-ups work better in lyric composition than in prose. Burroughs's *Nova Trilogy*, which features his most prominent use of the technique, remains largely unread. Given that cut-ups obliterate linear narrative, characterization, dramatic tension, and any type of coherent thought, readers can easily get capsized in the rushing torrent of disconnected words. The approach was apparently a freeing one for Burroughs, who believed that by dynamiting the structure of language itself, he could effectively "rub out the words" and reach a state of inner silence.

Bowie seems to have been one of the few to have actually read Burroughs's cut-up novels all the way through and gleaned something from them. Furthermore, the cut-ups became something to behold when alchemized by Bowie's own creative process. The songwriter's variation on the technique was to write a linear song, cut up the words and reassemble them, and then edit the resulting jumble back into something that had lyrical flow yet retained the startling juxtapositions provided by the process. Thus, on *Diamond Dogs*, *Low*, *"Heroes,"* and later works such as *Outside* and *Earthling*, Bowie's chopped-up lyrics project vivid emotional content—themes of paranoia, derangement, loss, and longing—through a fragmented lens. Largely freed from the trappings of linear narrative, the words and music are primed to make a direct connection to a receptive listener's unconscious mind. And the material's delivery agent is a tool that had been unavailable to Burroughs: melody.

Philosophically, Bowie and Burroughs were largely in sync. When the two first met, in 1974, they immediately bonded over a mutual disdain for the concept of love. "I gave too much of my time and energy to another person and they did the same to me and we started burning out against each other," Bowie said. "And that is what is termed love…that we decide to put all our values on another person. It's like two pedestals, each wanting to be the other pedestal."

"I don't think that 'love' is a useful word," Burroughs remarked.

Other points of convergence included their mutual disdain for the hippie movement, or for movements of any kind ("All this talk about a world family is a lot of bunk," Burroughs quipped), and a shared enthusiasm for pornography.

A primary theme running through much of Burroughs's writing is the desperate need to break free from all forms of control. This includes government control, societal control, the constricting control that comes from that part of ourselves ("the parasite," as Burroughs put it) that works against our best interests, even the controlling power of language itself. Bowie certainly sympathized with this aim, and it is telling that his first sustained use of the cut-up technique occurred on *Diamond Dogs*, an album that features several songs inspired by *Nineteen Eighty-Four*, George Orwell's great novel of individual freedom vs. an all-encompassing state. Bowie had tried, and failed, to secure rights from the Orwell estate to produce a full-length musical based on the book, but in songs like "Big Brother" and "1984" he still managed to convey Orwell's—and Burroughs's—themes of freedom vs. control loud and clear. That the record is tinged with an awareness of the futility of the struggle does not detract from the necessity of the fight.

Bowie's discovery of Burroughs and the cut-ups led slowly but inevitably to a trio of albums that continue to be regarded by many critics as the defining statement of his career, the so-called "Berlin Trilogy" of *Low*, *"Heroes,"* and *Lodger*, recorded in 1976, 1977, and 1978, respectively. The first two albums in particular convey the aural impression of stained glass that has been smashed and then carefully, though incorrectly, reassembled. Everything is a bit "off": Choruses arrive late or not at all; certain songs offer the promise of a dramatic build but then end without warning; in many cases, the expected vocals never appear, leaving the music to churn and bubble and glide along into a hazy sunset.

There is very little in the way of Nietzschean triumphalism on these albums. Instead, uncertainty predominates—perhaps most strikingly in the song "Always Crashing in the Same Car" (from *Low*), which, while lyrically inscrutable, conveys unmistakable feelings of lucklessness and inertia.

In such an atmosphere of doubt and brokenness, the song "Heroes," which is arguably Bowie's most mature distillation of his individualistic philosophy, stands in stark relief, its narrative coherence almost a rejoinder to the surrounding cut-ups. "Heroes" contains its share of obstacles both internal and external. Not only does the narrator "drink all the time," but he has to keep his love affair alive in a war-torn land in which "guns [are] shot above our heads" and a wall arbitrarily divides the population—a clear nod to the divided Berlin in which Bowie lived at the time of the song's composition. The song seems to echo the doomed love affair between Winston and Julia, the protagonists of *Nineteen Eighty-Four*, whose fledgling attempts at finding a personal space of joy and happiness are ultimately crushed by the all-seeing, all knowing Big Brother that rules Orwell's fictional future England.

As it turned out, Bowie had real-life models for his protagonists. From the window of the studio where he and the musicians worked on the album every day, he saw a young couple embrace in the shadow of the Berlin Wall, directly below a turret. Not only was he struck by the incongruity of this image, but he quickly realized that the couple in question consisted of Tony Visconti—Bowie's lifelong friend and the album's producer—and Antonia Maas, one of his backing singers. The fact that Visconti was limping through the last stages of a failing marriage at the time lent the situation an added poignancy—and futility.

Writer Nicholas Pegg notes that the song's elevation of the small and ordinary into the heroic signifies a move away from Bowie's Nietzschean Superman preoccupations into more nuanced territory. And yet, this is not quite the same as a naturalist's attempt to capture life as it is. "Heroes" is more akin to alchemy: We may be average and regular in the present moment, but we have the potential, at any time, for heroic thought and action—even if only for one day. The transformation can be brought about by an external event or through an internal change in perspective.

Bowie would never become a champion of the everyman in the vein of Springsteen, yet the narrator of "Heroes" is certainly more human, and consequently more accessible, than some of the icier figures of Bowie's earlier songs. And this, along with the song's soaring vocals and Robert Fripp's transcendent guitar work, goes a long way in explaining the longevity of "Heroes" It remains one of Bowie's most beloved, and most often-covered, compositions.

Bowie's music had always been distinctive, but in the Berlin Trilogy he created something wholly original. "These albums have song structures that were never designed before, production tricks that had never been used before, themes that had never been touched before, and a cool factor that absolutely cannot be beat," says screenwriter/musician Darren Callahan, one of the many artists of the succeeding generation to draw his inspiration from this period of Bowie's work.

> This music was parallel to, but never imitative of, punk rock, new wave, and disco, three of the most iconic periods in American music. Think of it: he DID NOT rip off these genres. You cannot say, "Hey, check out this awesome disco song by Bowie," in the way you might say that about "I Was Made For Lovin' You Baby" by KISS. He took all those forms (and others, like ambient music) and folded them into a completely original blend. No other period of his career was he so brave, so ahead of things, so absolutely free (and, let's be honest, so unhappy and drugged up). It is

> the only period, for me, where he is not calculating anything; he is truly just smoking the pipe of creativity, an absolute open channel with no regard for anyone.

A number of creative and personal factors contributed to the artistic breakthrough of the Berlin albums. In keyboardist/arranger Brian Eno, Bowie had found a kindred spirit, someone who was adventurous enough to extend the cut-ups beyond the realm of lyrics and into the music itself. Bowie and Eno would often compose sequences of music, write down the chords on notecards, shuffle them up, and then put the new sequences up on a bulletin board for the musicians to play. In many cases this resulted in discordant chaos, but not infrequently the exercise produced exciting new combinations that made their way onto the record.

With no regard for his record company's commercial considerations, Bowie opted to fill the second sides of both the *Low* and *"Heroes"* LPs with mostly instrumental music—an especially bold move given that most listeners gravitated to Bowie due to his dynamic singing. "*Low* and '*Heroes'* are really made for the LP experience," Callahan notes. "If you hear them on CD or streaming, the albums both seem to die out. But if you queued up Side 2 of *Low* and then put Side 2 of '*Heroes'* on the post, let them drop in that order on the turntable, it was one of the best ambient records of the '70s."

On the personal front, the Berlin Trilogy came at a point of crisis and transition. Finding himself addicted to cocaine and at an emotional dead end in Los Angeles by the mid-'70s, Bowie made the seemingly harebrained decision to move to Berlin ("the smack capital of Europe," he later remarked) with friend and fellow self-destructive rocker Iggy Pop, of all people, in an attempt to clean up his act. Bizarrely, his plan worked, though the recovery was gradual—its shaky trajectory charted over the course of the three albums. "The Berlin albums are the inner stage on which the crisis plays out," says *American Conservative* editor Daniel McCarthy, a longtime Bowie fan.

> They're emotionally powerful because they're a very conscious confrontation of Bowie with himself—he overcomes his afflictions not by rediscovering some purer, inner, more innocent figure but by carefully building a new persona that can express sympathy with other people's suffering—as heard on "Repetition" and "Fantastic Voyage" on *Lodger*, as well as on much of [post-Berlin release] *Scary Monsters*—even when he still feels set apart. It's not warm empathy for humanity that one finds on *Lodger* or *Scary Monsters* (or any later Bowie album), it's a sincere but cold simulation. He's thinking what he cannot feel, probably because after the introspection of *Low* he now understands just what he is and isn't capable of feeling.

Like Callahan, McCarthy regards the Berlin Trilogy (along with its immediate precursor and successor albums) as the pinnacle of Bowie's catalog, and refers to the accompanying persona of this period as "Weimar Bowie."

It's safe to say that Bowie's new approach baffled both his audience and the critics, even if the latter group ultimately came to regard these records as classics. Although his records routinely achieved platinum status in the past, Bowie's sales now hovered around 200,000. But if the albums alienated the general pop audience, they also attracted a new type of listener, best personified by the experimental composer Philip Glass, who was so taken with *Low* and *Heroes* that he went on to compose entire symphonies based around the albums twenty years later.

Here again Howard Roark comes to mind. He states in *The Fountainhead*, "I don't intend to build in order to have clients; I intend to have clients in order to build." This philosophy initially makes things very difficult for the architect. His first buildings are largely scorned by the establishment and the public. He is repeatedly brought to the very brink of financial ruin. But over time, certain like-minded individuals stumble upon his work: like-minded in the sense that they don't put stock in what the establishment or the public says about anything. Perhaps they drive by a gas station or house Roark designed, and it speaks to them. And these are the people who seek Roark out and become his small but loyal client base.

With the Berlin Trilogy, David Bowie built something new. And over time he attracted the right type of "clients." Younger acts such as Gary Numan, Devo (whom Bowie produced), Orchestral Manoeuvres in the Dark, The Human League, and virtually all of the

British "new pop" bands of the early 1980s picked up on Bowie's lead and extended the sound further. And contemporaries such as the Walker Brothers and Marianne Faithfull made radical course corrections in the wake of the music's release.

Bowie was certainly not the first, nor would he be the last, major pop star to take a bizarre left turn in the midst of a successful career. But he was relatively unique in his willingness to double down on his off-center ideas despite the drubbing he received. Most performers, when confronted with the cold shock of declining sales and an audience backlash, are quick to backpedal and return to the tried and true. Bowie, on the other hand, seemed to thrive on the animosity coming at him from all directions. If anything, it spurred him on to greater heights—a situation that would repeat itself almost exactly a decade later, and with arguably greater ferocity, during his foray with Tin Machine. In both instances his protracted intransigence put him at odds with his record label and led to a break—first with RCA at the end of the 1970s, then, at the end of the 1980s, with EMI, the very label that had rescued him. Tin Machine never did earn the respect Bowie felt it deserved, but in the case of the Berlin Trilogy he had the last laugh. In 1980 he released *Scary Monsters...And Super Creeps*, a bold and challenging album by any standard. But by that point audiences had caught up with him. The trilogy had already influenced key individuals in the nascent post-punk and new wave movements, who in turn had made inroads into the pop music mainstream, and so listeners were now more receptive to Bowie's chilly vocals; Robert Fripp's jagged, atonal riffs; and Visconti's treated drum sounds than they had been just three years ago. Also, Bowie's songs on this album, while still off-center, at least seemed to have choruses again. Audiences sighed in relief and bought the album by the truckload. *Scary Monsters* became a massive hit, and managed to vindicate its three predecessors in one fell swoop. Most important, it achieved this feat without compromise.

VIII

Want an axe to break the ice

Daniel McCarthy's earlier comments highlight an intriguing divergence between David Bowie the man and David Bowie the artist that began to occur after the release of *Scary Monsters*. Whether genuine or a "simulation" (as McCarthy feels), Bowie did begin to express—in interviews and occasionally in song—empathy for the sufferings of others as the new decade got underway, and this went hand in hand with newfound efforts to establish meaningful relationships in his life. Throughout the 1970s, David Bowie had embodied the Randian idea, as exemplified by Howard Roark's speech at the end of *The Fountainhead*, that "to a creator, all relations with men are secondary." That is, he lived for his art. His relationships, whether with session musicians, chauffeurs, groupies, or drug dealers, all tended to serve a utilitarian purpose. His views on love evolved during the decade, but it remained an emotion he wished to harness and control. "I think love is very important for my writing," he told Mavis Nicholson during their 1979 interview, but then added, "Love can't get quite in my way. I shelter myself from it incredibly."

Everything changed in the 1980s, partly due to Bowie's deepening relationship with his son. (He was awarded sole custody of Joey—who later reverted to his birth name of Duncan Jones—in his divorce from Angie.) Bowie evidently took stock of his way of living and found it lacking. He realized, as he later told Brett Anderson of Suede, "You do sacrifice a lot of real, honest, internal psychological safety by doing what we're doing."

> You end up as some sort of emotional casualty because you learn how to keep relationships away from you. And breaking that habit suddenly becomes very hard. You suddenly realize at some point that you don't have the equipment for creating relationships; because you've never utilized it, you don't know how to do it. You've lived your life learning how to not create relationships that will tie you down to anything or anybody. And there you are, at a certain age, thinking, "Wonder how you get to know people and develop something?"

So Bowie changed direction—drastically. This seems to have resulted, in the short run, in his becoming both a much happier person and a singularly uninteresting artist. His music, which had hitherto been so bold and edgy, quickly segued into a safe, pleasing affability to match his newly outgoing personality. Three albums—*Let's Dance, Tonight,* and *Never Let Me Down* came and went, racking up respectable positions on the charts. They were competent, well-crafted affairs, liked by many but loved by few.

The newfound warmth also led Bowie, perhaps inevitably, into the comforting cocoon of what Christopher Sandford terms "rock star liberalism." Bowie the Nietzschean had cared little for anything beyond the scope of his ambition. Bowie the fascist wanted to bend the world to his will. Bowie the ostensible human being did "story time for the local kids" during his sometime residency in the West Indies, according to his friend Mick Jagger, and "did a lot of work making health care better for local people."

Notably, Bowie remained opposed to publicly supporting causes until the end of his life. The few exceptions—his participation in the massive Live Aid concert for Ethiopian famine relief in 1985 and his later efforts to raise awareness of the routine, societally condoned abuse of women in Somalia—were the exceptions that proved the rule, and usually came about due to a personal connection. (In the former instance, he was lobbied heavily to participate in Live Aid by his friend Bob Geldof; in the latter instance, his newfound concern for the plight of Somalis was the direct result of his having married one: the model Iman Abdulmajid, his near-constant companion from 1991 until the end of his life.)

As a man, then, Bowie ceased to be a radical individual, at least of the type as defined by Ayn Rand. In fact, he repudiated the philosophies that had led him to ever become one. He became the ordinary man that Christopher Sandford believed had always comprised his true inner self: a sober, monogamous, easygoing fellow; a steadfastly heterosexual pillar of society who enjoyed quiet dinners with friends, quiet evenings in with the family, and who did his best to help those less fortunate. That was how it appeared anyway, though some credence is lent to Daniel McCarthy's theory that this too was a fabricated persona, by close scrutiny of Bowie's televised interviews from the 1990s and early 2000s: In segment after segment, the singer does a very good approximation of a contented middle-aged bloke, deliriously enthralled with domesticity. And yet the "offness" persists: the too-loud, seemingly arbitrary eruptions of laughter, the face-stretching grin that often segues into a leering grimace. These point to either a sustained act or barely suppressed anxiety. Or perhaps a little of both. All indications point to Bowie's contented family life in later years' being a reality, but it does not follow that the person who routinely put himself in front of cameras to tell charming stories while hawking product was the actual guy who tucked his daughter into bed at night. Most tellingly, Bowie seemed to tire of the charade and ceased doing interviews for the final decade of his life. He kept his private self private. In our current climate of overexposure, this can be viewed as a kind of radical act.

If Bowie's personal life ceased to resemble the strict Randian ideal we have been discussing, his artistic persona was a different matter, and this is where the Tin Machine experience proved transformative. From that point forward Bowie followed the dictates of his muse with every project. As an artist, he exemplified the Roark template right down the line. Reeves Gabrels summarized Bowie's creative process from this period in a tribute piece for *Mojo*: "Throughout the following 13 years [after *Tin Machine*], the studio was our Buckminster Fuller sandbox," Gabrels wrote. "Our safe place to create where time stopped and art was made. There was no careerism, or attention to a 'marketplace' but, instead, a desire to tell a story...leave a trail of good work."

A fair number of these records continue to divide critics, but at no point after 1988 could Bowie have been accused of phoning it in. In this writer's estimation, a sizable portion of his later work can stand alongside his '70s output without embarrassment. The 1995 album *Outside*, a reunion with Brian Eno, is not perfect—the music often teeters on the brink of chaos, and the half-baked narrative underlying this "non-linear Gothic Drama Hyper-Cycle" is distracting—but at its best moments it strikes out into exhilarating new territory: a madcap juxtaposition of classically tinged piano via Spiders-era sidekick Mike Garson, noise guitar from Reeves Gabrels, techno-influenced beats, with Bowie's voice floating eerily over the top—singing of madness and anxiety and the dislocating effects of technology. This is not the type of album one would have expected from a sober, happily married, middle-aged man. Bowie had figured out how to channel his lifelong anxieties concerning mental illness and isolation directly into his music, bypassing any need for the onetime pressure releases of drugs and promiscuous sexual behavior. Furthermore, he figured out a way to make such outpourings sound disconcertingly beautiful. He had achieved with his music what William Burroughs had intended, but failed to do, with the prose cut-ups: The work functioned as both effective self-therapy *and* satisfying art. And, like Tin Machine, *Outside* was a go-for-broke project. In the end, the album proved popular, but that almost seemed beside the point.

Writing in *Rolling Stone* shortly after Bowie's death, Trent Reznor, whose band Nine Inch Nails toured with Bowie in the mid-1990s, recalled how Bowie told him at the outset of their tour together, "I'm not going to play what anybody wants me to play. We're going to play a lot of *Low*-era-type things, and the new album. That's not what people are going to want to see. But that's what I need to do." Reznor confirmed that the audience reaction was indeed "subdued," bordering on hostile, but concluded, "That made an impression: In a world where the bar keeps seeming to be lower, where stupidity has got a foothold—there is still room for uncompromising vision."

In 2003 the Queen of England attempted to reward Bowie's lifetime of artistic excellence with a knighthood. Bowie refused, just as he had done with an earlier offer of a Commander of the British Empire (CBE) designation, stating "I would never have any intention of accepting anything like that. It's not what I spent my life working for." Thus he set himself apart from Sir Elton, Sir Mick, Sir Paul, Robert Plant CBE, and Jimmy Page OBE, all of whom, despite their supposedly renegade statuses, had lined up to receive their medals of approval from the British monarchy with alacrity.

Much has been made of Bowie's nearly decade-long retreat from public view toward the end of his life. There seemed to be several factors at play, calculation being the least of them. First, the retirement had its direct impetus in a heart attack Bowie suffered toward the end of his *Reality* tour in 2004. Just as he had made the decision to remove himself from his negative surroundings in Los Angeles in 1976, he came to the conclusion in the 2000s that a sustained life on the road was not conducive to his health. He also had a young daughter at home and wished to be more present during her early years than he had been for his son. But, perhaps most crucially from the public perspective, he simply did not feel he had anything more to say. Rather than simply push product out the door, as he had done with *Tonight* and *Never Let Me Down*, he stepped aside and let his legacy speak for itself.

Of course, that was not the end of the story. Bowie *did* return, triumphantly and entirely on his own terms, with the album *The Next Day* in 2013. The album functioned as a solid consolidation of his vision, touching on styles from throughout his career and connecting these disparate elements in a way that revealed their underlying consistency. He did no interviews and performed no concerts in support of the album, instead letting the work do the talking.

The Next Day received a favorable reaction from both audiences and critics. But most people concluded that even though Bowie was back and producing strong material, his days of creating entirely new sounds were behind him. No one was prepared, in other words, for *Blackstar*, his final album, released on January 8, 2016.

This album, like the Berlin Trilogy, can reasonably lay claim to having created a new genre. The foundations are based in free jazz—not surprising given that Bowie recruited a jazz ensemble led by New York musician Donny McCaslin to lay down much of the backing music. To this Bowie added his own stuttering guitar work, electronic treatments from various sources, and song structures that drew from krautrock, hip-hop, and other disparate genres. Tony Visconti tracked some of Bowie's vocals using an effect called ADT (automatic double-tracking) that gave them a disembodied, from-the-grave feel: a striking effect, given that many people first heard the material after Bowie died of cancer on January 10th.

It is not known how conscious Bowie was in the final few days of his life, and whether he had a chance to read Pitchfork Media's review, which stated, "This tortured immortality is no gimmick: Bowie will live on long after the man has died." One would hope that his mind was on other matters by that point. But he was fully in command of his faculties a week prior to his passing when he communicated with both Visconti and Eno via email and Skype. And so he would have already seen the avalanche of advance reviews declaring *Blackstar* his finest record since *Scary Monsters* and the Berlin Trilogy. He would surely have been gratified by Andy Gill's somewhat bemused characterization, in the *Independent*, of *Blackstar* as "the most extreme album of his entire career" and "as far as he's strayed from pop."

Thus having made his defining late-period statement, accompanied by an eerie video for the song "Lazarus" featuring the singer floating above a hospital bed, Bowie died. Only his family and a handful of collaborators had even known he was ill. It was one of the great final bows in pop music history. Even as the spark of life exited David Jones, *David Bowie*, the radical individualist, triumphed over death itself. He did indeed become Lazarus. This is the sort of ending Ayn Rand never thought to write for any of her characters, perhaps due to its spiritual aspect: the artist-hero making his exit—or his ascension—at the very peak of his creative powers, his final statement saturating public consciousness and causing all who came before him to look like amateurs simply because they lived and died without giving much thought to the presentation of the whole thing.

The body became spirit, and the spirit—that is, the art—lit up the planet.

IX

All the young dudes

It was stated earlier that Bowie came closer than any other massively popular entertainer to embodying the Randian artist-hero ideal. There are, of course, purer examples of this ideal to be found in the more obscure corners of rock and pop history. Take Mark Hollis, primary songwriter for the band Talk Talk, who said of that group's groundbreaking record *Spirit of Eden*, "For the people who recognize values in life, they need no further explanation of the record, they will intuitively understand. For the rest I will never explain." These words might as well have come from the mouth of Howard Roark. Hollis and his band were promptly sued by their label, EMI, for making "uncommercial music" around the same time that very label was at loggerheads with Bowie over Tin Machine. Hollis went on to make two more increasingly spare albums before disappearing entirely, leaving silence as his lasting statement.

Then there is David Sylvian, of the band Japan, who sits astride a solo catalog that is beautiful, uncompromising, and largely unheard. When Japan, who *had* enjoyed some commercial success in their distant past, reconvened in 1989–1990 to record new material, Sylvian insisted the outfit call itself Rain Tree Crow as a reflection of the group's new direction, even though such a move doomed their commercial prospects and frustrated the record label's hopes to capitalize on a reunion. Perhaps not surprisingly, Rain Tree Crow released just one album.

Relative to Bowie, these two artists labored in obscurity. But it is significant that they were both influenced by his Berlin Trilogy. And it is these artists, along with similarly fearless outside-looking-in acts such as Joy Division, The Cure, The Pixies, Nirvana, and Wilco that represent his true legacy. None of these artists consciously attempted to sound like Bowie. But all channeled his spirit of adventure, his willingness to experiment, and his willingness to stand by controversial decisions. Contrast these acts with Bowie's more obvious, and more imitative, heirs—Madonna, Lady Gaga, and Adam Lambert—and you will find the second group distinctly lacking.

That contrast between the surface-level imitators and the true heirs could not have been more apparent when Lady Gaga and Lorde performed posthumous tributes to David Bowie at the 2016 Grammy Awards and the Brit Awards, respectively. It is not an exaggeration to call Gaga's performance at the Grammys a desecration of his memory—in both spirit *and* presentation. It was the sort of easy-listening vaudeville atrocity Bowie had mocked his entire career: something akin to a Vegas-based Elton John impersonator in Bette Midler drag doing Bowie karaoke backed by slumming Cirque du Soleil dancers. On the other side of the Atlantic, performing with Bowie's own band, Lorde demonstrated an intuitive understanding of Bowie's primary takeaway: In her spare, haunting version of "Life on Mars," she made no effort to look or sound like Bowie. She performed as herself.

In his *Mojo* piece, Reeves Gabrels stated:

> It is my deepest hope that David is remembered as a man and an artist and not turned into a once-upon-a-time symbol of controversy by the media, a saucy soundbite by the tabloids or a silkscreen on a t-shirt worn by baby boomers and hipsters alike trying to create the appearance of cool without ever looking below the surface.

What is Lady Gaga if not a living silkscreen of Bowie? Speaking to *The Hollywood Reporter* just a few days before Bowie's death, she gave a grammatically confused explanation of her adoration that missed the intent—and, indeed, the entire content—of his work:

> When I fell in love with David Bowie, when I was living on the Lower East Side, I always felt that his glamor was something he was using to express a message to people that was very healing for their souls. He is a true, true artist and I don't know if I ever went, "Oh, I'm going to be that way like this," or if I arrived upon it slowly, realizing it was my calling and that's what drew me to him.

What's frustrating is that Lady Gaga is a musician of some talent. She is in all likelihood a technically far superior musician to Lorde. But that talent has rarely translated into songs of any lasting merit. The promise on display on her first album has been largely absent on subsequent efforts. It's clear that she has a good heart, what with her various foundations and anti-bullying campaigns and the like, but she lacks the intellectual depth or overarching ethos that animated Bowie even during his most fallow periods.

Madonna is almost the inverse. She has something approaching the intellectual depth but she largely lacks the talent. Her own online tribute demonstrated at least some familiarity with Bowie's actual music: "His lyrics were witty, ironic and mysterious," she wrote. "At the time (I first saw him) he was the Thin White Duke and he had mime artists on stage with him and very specific choreography. And I saw how he created a persona and used different art forms within the arena of Rock and Roll to create entertainment. I found him so inspiring and innovative. Unique and provocative. A real Genius."

Madonna made a massive impact on popular culture in her day. Nothing can take that away from her. The problem is this: How many great albums has Madonna actually made? Two, tops? How many Madonna songs will be in regular rotation fifty years from now? Where are her equivalents to "Space Oddity," "The Man Who Sold the World," "Changes," "Life on Mars," "Rebel Rebel," "Fame," "Heroes," and "Ashes to Ashes"? She may have a few in striking distance of "Let's Dance" but that's about it.

Perhaps Bowie's only legitimate heir in terms of a longstanding mega-popular artist was Prince, who sadly passed away on April 21, 2016. Like the alternative acts mentioned earlier, Prince never tried to sound like Bowie. He covered Bowie's material on a handful of occasions: first in 2014 with a live rendition of "Let's Dance." Then, on what turned out to be his final tour, he performed a haunting, reworked version of "Heroes" at least twice, most notably during his last-ever performance on April 14. Privately, he is known to have admired Bowie and enjoyed singing Bowie's songs to friends. The two met in 1987, when Prince invited Bowie to his Paisley Park complex and played him the then unreleased *Black Album* in its entirety. In terms of theatricality, "gender fluidity," image shifting, sartorial extravagance, and, of course, originality and quality of material, Prince arguably carried the baton forward within his *own* self-created genre in spectacular fashion. Radical individualism? Few would challenge the notion that Prince possessed this trait in spades.

    The fact that there was just the one discernible heir in the pop music mainstream (if we except Nirvana, who violently removed themselves from the conversation with Kurt Cobain's suicide in 1994), and now, sadly, there are none, is perhaps appropriate. Only the extraordinary are capable of reaching the bar Bowie (and, later, Prince) set. And there are not many of such types out there.

What can we learn from David Bowie? Simply that we can be heroes; that we ought to rise above mediocrity; that there is a place in life for style and professionalism; that "the gift of sound and vision" is exactly that, and more of us ought to start thinking about what our own vision might be.

    At the 2016 Brit Awards, Gary Oldman said of his departed friend, "Whether in music or in life, [Bowie] emphasized originality, experimentation, exploration, and in his very unique way, he also reminded us to never take ourselves too seriously." He added, "David, you were mortal, but your potential was superhuman."

There is little chance that the masses will recognize such potential in themselves anytime soon. But for the exceptional few, David Bowie's life and work have issued a challenge. It's time to go meet it.

Epilogue

Ten Individualist Bowie Tracks: A Playlist

Throughout this book I have highlighted a number of Bowie's songs that showcase his individualist philosophy. These include "Rebel Rebel," "Heroes," "Changes," "Oh! You Pretty Things," and "Cygnet Committee." What follows is a playlist of ten additional tracks, selected in consultation with my friend and fellow Bowiephile Daniel McCarthy. As editor of *The American Conservative* and former Internet Communications Director for Ron Paul's 2008 presidential campaign, Daniel is uniquely qualified to speak to Bowie's social-libertarian themes, and I have included a number of his insights in the capsule synopses below.

1. **Up the Hill Backwards (*Scary Monsters*, 1980):** "The vacuum created by the arrival of freedom / and the possibilities, if one can grasp it." In this opening couplet, Bowie gives voice to both the Burkean and radical libertarian impulses, acknowledging the dislocation, or "vacuum," created by the upending of established mores while at the same time welcoming the "possibilities" that such a shift heralds. This sentiment is echoed in the chorus, in which society is described as moving "up the hill backwards." In a note of guarded optimism, we are told that "it'll be all right."

2. **Panic in Detroit (*Aladdin Sane*, 1973):** Like "Cygnet Committee," this song eviscerates violent

political revolutionaries. The unnamed central character, who "looks a lot like Che Guevara" and is "the only survivor of the National People's Gang," sits out a riot he has instigated and ends up dead, presumably by his own hand, at song's end. "My guess is that Bowie really was put off by the idiocy of rioting," McCarthy observes, "and certainly didn't see anything revolutionary, progressive, or liberating about it."

3. Jump They Say (*Black Tie, White Noise*, 1993): This is Bowie's most direct attempt to come to grips with his half-brother Terry Burns' long-term struggle with mental illness and ultimate suicide. Here he casts Burns as a heroic figure, condemned at every turn for being different. "They" tell Burns to "jump"—a double entendre, surely: It can be taken to mean both "jump on command" and "jump off the roof." Bowie, on the other hand, implores his brother to not listen to such commands. "I take this to be about ignoring the crowd as well as the negative voices in your head," McCarthy says, "even though it didn't work out for Bowie's brother."

4. All the Madman (*The Man Who Sold the World*, 1970): An earlier, more overtly nightmarish treatment of the same subject, in which the inmates of an asylum are portrayed as being saner than those outside. "I'd rather stay here with all the madmen than perish with the sad men who roam free," Bowie sings.

5. Loving the Alien (*Tonight*, 1984) and **6. Young Americans (*Young Americans*, 1975)**: "What I'm really struck by in these two songs is Bowie's genius for affectionate ambiguity," McCarthy states. "Neither of these is a straightforward manifesto. 'Loving the Alien,' on its surface, emphasizes common humanity in a critique of organized religion. But just imagine how awful it would be if someone with Richard Dawkins's sensibility had written it. 'Young Americans' winds up being a celebration of young Americans even though the lyrics are about unfulfilling sex, 'bills you have to pay,' and President Nixon—because somehow the idea of aspiration and dreaming of making it big are still part of the song's undercurrent. It's very subtle. In these songs, Bowie seems to make a critical point through the eyes of a participant, and the participant is never self-hating despite the critique: It's still good to be a young American despite the conditions of the '70s; it's still good to be a believer even though you know the problems religion can cause. Bowie isn't directly affirming either of these perspectives, of course, but he's looking at them all through a participant's eyes, so the critique is not outside and absolute."

7. The Next Day (*The Next Day*, 2013): This has been perceived by some to be a critique of Christianity, though it could just as easily be interpreted as a condemnation of the religious authorities of the day from Christ's perspective. In either case, the song defends a visionary against a corrupt authority. "First they give you everything that you want / Then they take back everything that you have," Bowie sings. Here, freedom comes with strings attached.

8. Watch That Man (*Aladdin Sane*, 1973): Showcases the "sheer transgressive hedonistic sides of rock-n-roll and libertarianism," McCarthy says. "It's the *Reason* magazine of Bowie songs."

9. Joe the Lion (*"Heroes,"* 1977): Celebrates performance artist Chris Burden, a most radical individual indeed. As per the lyrics, Burden had himself nailed to his car, in a crucifixion pose, for his piece *Trans-Fixed*. The line "Guess you'll buy a gun," refers to the piece *Shoot*, in which Burden was shot in the arm by an assistant. This "man of iron" died in 2015 at the relatively advanced age of 69.

10. Red Sails (*Lodger*, 1978): Selected by McCarthy "because libertarians like pirates."

Acknowledgments

This book owes its existence to the efforts of my good friend John J. Miller. Shortly after Bowie died, John asked if I might consider writing something in tribute, similar to a piece I had done on Lou Reed for *National Review Online*. When it became apparent, owing to my decades-long obsession with Bowie, that this new work would need to be longer and more considered, John put me in touch with Liberty Island Media. His unwavering enthusiasm for the proposed project played no small part in its coming to pass. For his encouragement in this and many other endeavors, I remain eternally grateful.

It has been a pleasure to work with Adam Bellow, David S. Bernstein, David Swindle, and Elena Vega at Liberty Island. Their thoroughness and professionalism continue to impress me deeply.

Christopher Sandford, one of the all-time great music journalists, has been a source of inspiration and guidance. His characterization of Bowie as a circumspect introvert proved, for me, the key that cracked the code. I suspect that I may harbor a more besotted view of Mr. Bowie than Christopher, but if I have managed at all to convey some evenhandedness and objectivity in this narrative, I owe that achievement to his example.

I would like to thank Darren Callahan, Richard Kaczynski, Daniel McCarthy, Mike Richmond, Bret Helm, and J.R. Parker for their invaluable insights, many of which have made their way into the text.

Some of the Crowley and Burroughs material in these pages hearkens back to pieces I originally wrote for *Blurt* magazine. I remain deeply indebted to Stephen Judge and Fred Mills for their assistance with that earlier work.

Finally, I owe my largest debt of gratitude to my wife, Harper Piver, for her encouragement, support, and accommodation. Our daughter is not yet old enough to read this book, but perhaps someday she will peruse its pages for some understanding of what all the fuss was about.

Viva la Thin White Duke.

Robert Lurie
04/18/2016

Sources

Bebergal, Peter. *Season of the Witch: How the Occult Saved Rock and Roll.* New York: Tarcher/Penguin, 2014.

Blehar, Jeffrey. "David Bowie: Renaissance Man." *National Review Online*, 13 Jan. 2016. Web. 14 Mar. 2016. <http://www.nationalreview.com/article/429736/david-bowies-renaissance-man-legacy>.

Booth, Martin. *A Magick Life: A Biography of Aleister Crowley.* London: Coronet, 2001.

Brink, Rebecca Vipond. "Let's Talk About David Bowie's Predation (And The Online Conversation Surrounding It)" *The Frisky.* 14 Jan. 2016. Web. 01 Mar. 2016. <http://www.thefrisky.com/2016-01-14/lets-talk-about-david-bowies-predation-and-the-online-conversation-surrounding-it/>.

Buckley, David. *Strange Fascination: David Bowie: The Definitive Story.* London: Virgin, 2005

Burroughs, William S. *The Adding Machine: Selected Essays.* New York: Arcade, 1993.

Burroughs, William S. *Rub Out the Words: The Letters of William S. Burroughs 1959-1974.* New York: Ecco, 2012.

David Bowie in His Own Words: Interviews and Contributions. Perf. David Bowie. I.V. Media, 2015. DVD.

"David Bowie-The Lord's Prayer, Sleep In Heavenly Peace." YouTube. *YouTube,* 11 Jan. 2016. Web. 01 Mar. 2016. <https://www.youtube.com/watch?v=RGd-wNOq8d4>.

Copetas, Greg. "Beat Godfather Meets Glitter Mainman." *Rolling Stone,* 28 Feb. 1974.

"David Bowie Interview." Interview by Karel De Graaf. *Karel.* Dutch Television. Amsterdam, 29 Jan. 1996. Television.

"David Bowie Interview." Interview by Mavis Nicholson. *Afternoon Plus.* Thames Television. London, 16 Feb. 1979. Television.

Crowley, Aleister. "Liber LXXVII." *Hermetic Library.* Ordo Templi Orientis, n.d. Web. 13 Jan. 2016. <http://hermetic.com/crowley/libers/lib77.html>.

Doggett, Peter. "The Fall To Earth: David Bowie, Cocaine And The Occult." *The Quietus.* 11 Jan. 2016. Web. 01 Feb. 2016. <http://thequietus.com/articles/07233-david-bowie-cocaine-low>.

Doino, William J. "David Bowie's Search for God." *First Things*, Feb. 2016. Web. 14 Mar. 2016. <https://www.firstthings.com/web-exclusives/2016/02/david-bowies-search-for-god>.

Dombal, Ryan. "Blackstar." David Bowie: Album Review. *Pitchfork Media,* 06 Jan. 2016. Web. 19 Apr. 2016. <http://pitchfork.com/reviews/albums/21332-blackstar/>.

Durant, Will, and Ariel Durant. *The Lessons of History.* May 27, 2004. Read by Grover Gardner with with commentary by Will Durant and Ariel Durant. Blackstone Audio, 7 June 2004. Compact Disc.

Egan, Sean, and David Bowie. *Bowie on Bowie: Interviews and Encounters with David Bowie.* Chicago: Chicago Review, 2015.

"Friedrich Nietzsche." *Wikipedia.* Wikimedia Foundation, n.d. Web. 15 Feb. 2016. <https://en.wikipedia.org/wiki/Friedrich_Nietzsche>.

Gill, Andy. "David Bowie: Blackstar." *The Independent.* Independent Digital News and Media, 06 Jan. 2016. Web. 01 Mar. 2016. <http://www.independent.co.uk/arts-entertainment/music/reviews/david-bowies-blackstar-exclusive-first-review-a-bowie-

desperate-to-break-with-the-past-a6783456.html>.

Gilmore, Mikal. "David Bowie: 1947-2016." *Rolling Stone,* 11 Feb. 2016.

Greene, Andy. "The Inside Story of David Bowie's Stunning New Album, 'Blackstar'" *Rolling Stone.* 23 Nov. 2015. Web. 01 Mar. 2016. <http://www.rollingstone.com/music/features/the-inside-story-of-david-bowies-stunning-new-album-blackstar-20151123>.

Hann, Michael. "Just Say No: 10 Things David Bowie Turned down." *The Guardian.* Guardian News and Media, 19 Feb. 2016. Web. 12 Mar. 2016. <http://www.theguardian.com/music/musicblog/2016/feb/19/david-bowie-dave-grohl-coldplay-10-things-turned-down>.

Head, Alec A. "Rain Tree Crow." *Satan Stole My Teddy Bear.* 01 Feb. 2011. Web. 20 Apr. 2016. <http://www.ssmt-reviews.com/artist/rain_tree_crow.html>.

Hiatt, Brian. "The Final Years: How Bowie stepped away – and came roaring back." *Rolling Stone,* 11 Feb. 2016.

Hochman, David. "Playboy Interview: Gary Oldman." *Playboy.com.* 25 June 2014. Web. 14 Mar. 2016.

<https://www.playboy.com/articles/gary-oldman-playboy-interview>.

Jagger, Mick. "Mick Jagger Remembers David Bowie: 'He Would Share So Much With Me'" *Rolling Stone*. 26 Jan. 2016. Web. 01 Mar. 2016. <http://www.rollingstone.com/music/news/mick-jagger-remembers-david-bowie-he-would-share-so-much-with-me-20160126>.

"Jean-Jacques Rousseau." *Wikipedia*. Wikimedia Foundation, n.d. Web. 15 Feb. 2016. <https://en.wikipedia.org/wiki/Jean-Jacques_Rousseau>.

Kaczynski, Richard. *Perdurabo: The Life of Aleister Crowley*. Berkeley: North Atlantic, 2010.

Katz, Jessica. "Lady Gaga Describes When She 'Fell In Love With David Bowie'" *Billboard*. 11 Jan. 2016. Web. 14 Mar. 2016. <http://www.billboard.com/articles/news/6836536/lady-gaga-describes-love-david-bowie>.

Kirk, Russell. *The Conservative Mind: From Burke to Eliot*. Washington, D.C.: Regnery, 2001.

Loder, Kurt. "David Bowie: Straight Time." *Rolling Stone*. 12 May 1983.

Mattix, Lori, as told to Michael Kaplan. "I Lost My Virginity to David Bowie." *Thrillist*. N.p., 27 Oct. 2015. Web. 01 Mar. 2016.

<https://www.thrillist.com/entertainment/nation/i-lost-my-virginity-to-david-bowie>.

Morgan, Ted. *Literary Outlaw: The Life and Times of William S. Burroughs.* New York: Avon, 1990.

"The Next Day The Day After." *davidbowie.com*. 10 May 2013. Web. 14 Mar. 2016. <http://www.davidbowie.com/news/next-day-day-after-51651>.

Nietzsche, Friedrich. *Twilight of the Idols / The Anti-Christ.* New York: Penguin, 1990.

Orwell, George. *Nineteen Eighty-four: A Novel.* New York: Harcourt, Brace, 1949.

Pearson, Keith Ansell. *How to Read Nietzsche.* New York: W.W. Norton & Company, 2005.

Pegg, Nicholas. *The Complete David Bowie.* London: Titan, 2011.

Pennington, Louise. "David Bowie, Jimmy Page and That Small Issue of Child Rape." *LousiePennington.org,* 11 Jan. 2016. Web. 01 Mar. 2016. <http://louisepennington.org/david-bowie-jimmy-page-and-that-small-issue-of-child-rape/>.

Rand, Ayn. *The Fountainhead.* New York: Signet, 1968.

Rand, Ayn. *The Romantic Manifesto: A Philosophy of Literature.* New York: Signet, 1975.

"Reeves Gabrels On Creating With Bowie." *MOJO.* 08 Feb. 2016. Web. 14 Mar. 2016. <http://www.mojo4music.com/23108/reeves-gabrels-on-creating-with-bowie-the-studio-was-our-sandbox/>.

Reznor, Trent. "Trent Reznor Recalls How David Bowie Helped Him Get Sober." *Rolling Stone,* http://www.rollingstone.com/music/news/trent-reznor-recalls-how-david-bowie-helped-him-get-sober-20160126, January 26, 2016.

Salerno, Joseph T. "David Bowie, RIP." *Mises Wire.* The Mises Institute, 11 Jan. 2016. Web. 18 Apr. 2016. <https://mises.org/blog/david-bowie-rip-0>.

Sandford, Christopher. *Bowie: Loving the Alien.* New York: Da Capo Press, 1998.

Sandford, Christopher. "Thin Right Duke." *The American Conservative,* March/April 2016.

Shepherd, Jack. "Read Gary Oldman's Emotional Brits Tribute to David Bowie in Full." *The Independent.* Independent Digital News and Media, 25 Feb. 2016. Web. 14 Mar. 2016. <http://www.independent.co.uk/arts-entertainment/music/news/david-bowie-brit-

awards-2016-gary-oldman-emotional-tribute-in-full-a6894881.html>.

"Spirit of Eden." *Snow In Berlin:* N.d. Web. 14 Mar. 2016. <http://www.snowinberlin.com/spiritofeden.html>.

Timberg, Scott. "David Bowie, Rock Star Groupies and the Sexually Adventurous '70s: "Labeling Us as Victims in Retrospect Is Not a Very Conscious Thing to Do"." *Salon.* N.d. Web. 01 Mar. 2016. <http://www.salon.com/2016/01/13/david_bowie_rock_star_groupies_and_the_sexually_adventurous_70s_labeling_us_as_victims_in_retrospect_is_not_a_very_conscious_thing_to_do/>.

Tremlett, George. *David Bowie: Living on the Brink.* New York: Carroll & Graf, 1996.

Williams, Stereo. "David Bowie and Rock 'n' Roll's Statutory Rape Problem." *The Daily Beast.* Newsweek/Daily Beast, 16 Jan. 2016. Web. 01 Mar. 2016. <http://www.thedailybeast.com/articles/2016/01/17/david-bowie-and-rock-n-roll-s-statutory-rape-problem.html>.

ABOUT THE AUTHOR

Robert Dean Lurie is a writer and musician based in Tempe, Arizona. He received his MFA in Creative Writing from the University of North Carolina Wilmington and is the author of *No Certainty Attached: Steve Kilbey* and

The Church (Verse Chorus Press, 2009) and co-author (with Ray Fisher) of *The Edge: Life Lessons From a Martial Arts Master* (CreateSpace, 2013). His essays on arts and culture have appeared in National Review, Blurt Magazine, The American Conservative, Crux Literary Journal, Front Porch Republic, and Chronicles.

Printed in Great Britain
by Amazon